Table Talk
Volume 1

Devotions

TABLE TALK:
Bible Stories You Should Know
Volume 1

Pastor's Program Kit

Pastor's Program Guide (kit only)

Resource CD-ROM (kit only)

Plus one each of the components listed below:

Devotions

Teen Talk: Youth Leader Guide

Small Talk: Children's Leader Guide

Table Topper Signs (Pack of 30)

Carl Frazier

TABLE TALK

Bible Stories You Should Know

VOLUME 1

DEVOTIONS BY BEN SIMPSON

Abingdon Press
Nashville

Carl Frazier

TABLE TALK:
Bible Stories You Should Know
Volume 1

Devotions
by Ben Simpson

ISBN 978-1-4267-5800-3

Scripture quotations, unless otherwise indicated, are from the Common English Bible, copyright © 2010 by Common English Bible, and are used by permission.

Scripture quotations marked NIV are taken from the Holy Bible, NEW INTERNATIONAL VERSION®, NIV®. © 1973, 1978, 1984 by Biblica, Inc.™ Used by permission of Zondervan. All rights reserved worldwide.

Scripture quotations marked KJV are from the King James or Authorized Version of the Bible.

Library of Congress Cataloging-in-Publication applied for.

13 14 15 16 17 18 19 20 21 22—10 9 8 7 6 5 4 3 2 1

MANUFACTURED IN THE UNITED STATES OF AMERICA

Contents

Introduction

The Bible is a glorious book, filled with stories that all of us should know. As the author of 2 Timothy 3:16-17 writes, "Every scripture is inspired by God and is useful for teaching, for showing mistakes, for correcting, and for training character, so that the person who belongs to God can be equipped to do everything that is good."

Do you belong to God, or think you might want to? Do you want to "be equipped to do everything that is good"? Then the Bible has much to offer you. In addition to the uses listed above, the Bible contains all things necessary that we might "be wise in a way that leads to salvation through faith that is in Christ Jesus" (2 Timothy 3:15). Christians believe that the Bible points ultimately to Jesus and that through its words we encounter him, come to know him, and grow as his disciples. The Bible is not just filled with stories you should know; it is an introduction to a person you should know.

If you are a beginner in the study of the Bible, be patient with the text and with yourself. The Bible is a collection of sixty-six books, thirty-nine in the Old Testament and twenty-seven in the New Testament. It is a complex but understandable book. Though the culture and customs of the people we encounter within its pages may seem distant to us, many of their experiences will be familiar. Through diligent study and the help of able teachers, you will profit as you grow in knowledge. Stay with it.

I hope that those of you who have been studying the Bible for many years will come to the text with an open mind and a teachable heart. As you likely have discovered through devoted study, old stories take on fresh meanings from time to time. God may have something new to teach you; may you be prepared to listen.

How to Use This Book

This devotional guide was written to accompany Volume 1 of *Table Talk: Bible Stories You Should Know*, by Carl Frazier. The guide follows the structure of the Table Talk program, providing reflection on the six Bible stories explored in this volume over a six-week period. The stories in Volume 1 are:

1. Creation (the Creation accounts of Genesis 1)
2. The Fall (the temptation story of Genesis 3)
3. The Flood (the story of Noah and the Great Flood found in Genesis 6–9)
4. Father Abraham (an overview of the life of Abraham in Genesis 12, 15, and 22)
5. Ten Words (the Ten Commandments, as described in Exodus 20)
6. The Great Commandment (as spoken by Moses in Deuteronomy 6)

Each of the six weeks receives six daily devotions followed by a seventh entry called "Living the Story," in which readers are encouraged to move from meditation to action.

This book of devotions can be used by individuals, by families studying Scripture together, or by groups of people seeking to spur one another on in faith. For families with young children, you may wish to prepare for your time together by reading the entry and anticipating questions your children may have.

Though these devotions were written to accompany the Table Talk program, they can also stand on their own. Anyone seeking God will benefit from the practice of Bible reading, contemplation, and prayer. It is my hope these reflections will connect you to the God revealed in Jesus Christ and that you may come to know and follow God.

Experience the Power of the Bible

The Bible serves many purposes. I will share two of these. First, the Bible is meant to invade our imaginations and invite us into God's story. In this respect, the texts of the Bible are narratives, or stories, and stories they must remain. Fresh readings will yield new possibilities and applications as contexts and circumstances change. These stories are never truly mastered. Instead, we become mastered by them and by the God who stands above them, giving inspiration and life to the words.

Second, these stories are meant to convey important ideas. These ideas have been explored for generations by pastors, theologians, and ordinary people like you and me. They have yet to be exhausted, though strong and convincing conclusions have been reached. The meditations in this book by no means express the final theological authority on these texts, though I have diligently sought to lean on and incorporate reliable voices.

In addition, the readings are meant to inspire fresh thinking, deepen love for God, and motivate the faithful to action in our world. It is my prayer that each entry accomplishes all three aims, but if not, don't miss the message due to the shortcomings of the messenger. God has given us the Bible so that we might come to know the Father, Son, and Holy Spirit, and I trust that that will occur. Through these meditations, I hope you will dedicate yourself to greater engagement with God, and to the larger conversation called theology.

A cornerstone for the work of theology is knowledge of the Bible. I am so glad you have chosen to study this book and discuss its meaning with others, and I am sure you will grow in your confidence as you learn what the Bible contains. One of my teachers, Howard Hendricks, has stated:

> There's nothing like the self-assurance that comes from firsthand knowledge of the Bible. It gives you confidence to think for yourself. Most people don't think—they merely rearrange their prejudices. But it's altogether different when you know what the Bible says, where it says it, and what it means. That kind of personal ownership of spiritual truth cuts you free from the leash of popular opinion.[1]

Read these Bible stories; learn what they say, where they are found, and what they mean. Then live the story, to the glory of God.

Week One
CREATION

Genesis 1:1–2:4a

1. BRINGING FORTH BEAUTY

When God began to create the heavens and the earth—the earth
was without shape or form, it was dark over the deep sea, and
God's wind swept over the waters—God said, "Let there be
light." And so light appeared. (Genesis 1:1-3)

The Genesis 1 Creation story states this historical fact: God
shaped and formed the world, and brought it into being. But the
story is first poetry, declaring universal truths about God's why
behind the text. As Robert Frost wrote, "The utmost of ambition
is to lodge a few poems where they will be hard to get rid of."[2] In
Genesis 1, we have just such a poem.

Verses 1-3, quoted above, tell us that God brought order from
chaos. God spoke, and it was so. The word of God is a powerful
thing. Just as we anticipate what God brings forth when we read

the Genesis 1 narrative, we wait for that moment when the Word speaks to us, and takes the mess and muck of our struggles to bring forth beauty and wholeness and peace.

The power of God's creative word, expressed at the beginning of Genesis and repeated throughout this poetic description of the Creation, inspires awe. Who knew that such a God exists, a God who creatively crafts our world according to divine purposes, loving and caring and expressing concern for all we encounter? The story declares there is a God who has created in order to be in relationship to the world that was shaped and formed from darkness, chaos, and nothingness. With a word, God has brought forth all that is, including you.

Creator God, provide me the grace I need to recognize when you are at work. Take the raw material of my life, send forth your Spirit, and put me together. Help me to look to you as the one who brings order and wholeness, completeness and peace. As you brought forth light with a word, cutting through darkness at the beginning of your creative work, place and call forth your light within me, that I might shine before others, bringing glory to you. Amen.

2. GOD TAKES NOTICE

When I look up at your skies, at what your fingers made—the moon and the stars that you set firmly in place—what are human beings that you think about them; what are human beings that you pay attention to them? You've made them only slightly less than divine, crowning them with glory and grandeur.
(Psalm 8:3-5)

When I was a boy, my father took me hunting in the hill country of Texas, far from home and the normal rhythms of life. We slept on old bunks in a tin shack with other men from our family. Our meals were prepared on an old gas stove, lanterns and flashlights lit our way at night, wood-burning stoves kept us warm, and the plumbing did not work well, if at all.

Each evening, we stepped outside the shack and used water drawn from a well to brush our teeth, standing beneath the stars. Oh, so many stars! Ten-year-old me felt small. Underneath such an expanse, who am I? And does God take notice of my little life?

The psalmist's words precede my experience by thousands of years, but the concern is the same. As you recall, Genesis 1 describes God's creative action: God spoke, and it was so. Light and darkness, ocean and sky, land and vegetation, heavenly lights, animal life, and finally human beings were brought into being by the power of the divine Word.

The psalmist draws our gaze upward to the vastness of our world, while calling us to glance within, reflecting through comparison on our small magnificence. God created all this! And you and me. Small though we may be, God takes notice and gives us a place of honor in the created order. We are called to know the God who brought us into being and to live responsibly and faithfully as God's creatures.

God of all that is made, I am small in comparison to this great big world. But you know me, you have made me, and you have called me. You have placed your Spirit upon me, by the grace of your Son, Jesus Christ. You have purposed me for great things in your service. You love me. May I be humbled by this reality, and may my love for you grow. Amen.

3. A Gift and a Responsibility

Then God said, "Let us make humanity in our image to resemble us so that they may take charge of the fish of the sea, the birds of the sky, the livestock, all the earth, and all the crawling things on earth." God created humanity in God's own image, in the divine image God created them, male and female God created them. (Genesis 1:26-27)

When I was a teenager, a friend and I operated a lawn service. Each summer we worked hard under the hot sun, believing the heat toughened us up for the fall football season.

During that experience, I learned something about the importance of how we represent others, and how our identity extends beyond ourselves. One of our customers, who happened to know my father, was disappointed with the service we provided. Suddenly, it was not only my name that hung in the balance, but my father's as well. He shared with me the importance of the Simpson name, for it represented something not only about me, but about our family as well.

In Genesis 1, God created humanity "in God's own image." Both male and female bear the image of God. In a divine, magnificent way, God has placed a stamp on each of our lives, marking us as distinct from the rest of creation, giving human beings a responsibility to steward and care for all that has been made.

When we live as God intends, we represent something, or someone, beyond ourselves. Living as disciples of Jesus Christ leads us more fully to reflect God's person and reality before other human beings, calling them to realize that they too are known and loved by the God who brought this world into being.

O God, in whose image I am made, may I see that you have placed upon me your mark. I represent not only myself but also you, for in some way my life reflects your being. May I represent you well, and may you, by your grace, go about the work needed to remake and repair me where I do not follow you faithfully. Amen.

4. HOME MAINTENANCE

God blessed them and said to them, "Be fertile and multiply;
fill the earth and master it. Take charge of the fish of the sea,
the birds of the sky, and everything crawling on the ground."
Then God said, "I now give to you all the plants on the earth
that yield seeds and all the trees whose fruit produces its seeds
within it. These will be your food. To all wildlife, to all the birds
of the sky, and to everything crawling on the ground—to every-
thing that breathes—I give all the green grasses for food." And
that's what happened. God saw everything he had made:
it was supremely good. (Genesis 1:28-31a)

Several years ago, my wife and I became homeowners. Our house was built in the 1960s and had begun to show its age. Windows needed replacing, and new paint, electrical work, and yard maintenance were necessary. Our corner of the created order required constant care, and we became responsible.

Following the creation of people in Genesis 1, God handed out responsibilities. God told human beings to "be fertile and multiply." God said to "take charge" over the animals, the birds, and the insects—over all living things. God declared the vegetation would provide food. And God looked upon all that was made and saw "it was supremely good."

These words from Genesis are a call God issues to us—to steward and care for creation. We are called to manage our food resources wisely, to advocate for creation, to preserve wildlife, to ensure the continued fruitfulness of the land, and to protect the ecosystem from ruin. "Environmentalism" is not a cause, but a mandate from the Creator.

In addition, we are called to beautify our communities and nurture life. My own family sees the care of our home, and the parcel of land surrounding it, as a trust given by God to be maintained and nurtured for our use, and also for the benefit of the community—our neighbors and our successors.

Look at all God has made; it is "supremely good." Care for it, as God commands.

Ruler of Creation, thank you for calling me to be a steward of all you have made. May I be responsible and engaged with this world, playing the part you have given me in the health and flourishing of all that is. Amen.

5. The Creator, the Created, and Christ

Jesus came near and spoke to them, "I've received all authority in heaven and on earth. Therefore, go and make disciples of all nations, baptizing them in the name of the Father and of the Son and of the Holy Spirit, teaching them to obey everything that I've commanded you. Look, I myself will be with you every day until the end of this present age." (Matthew 28:18-20)

The Genesis stories tell us that God is the Lord of all the earth. Then, in Matthew 28, Jesus completed and extended the picture by stating that he had received "all authority in heaven and on earth." On the basis of that declaration, Jesus issued a commission. He gave his disciples responsibilities. They were to go to every nation under heaven, and to teach human beings to obey everything Jesus had commanded.

Notice that Jesus' words in Matthew are directed not just to the eleven who initially heard the words, but also to all who come after them, until the end of the age. As you walk through the winding wood near your home, as you gaze up at the stars, as you marvel at the creatures of the wilderness and the birds of the air, Jesus is near—present and attentive.

19

Accepting the statement that God created the world is a step in the right direction. But understanding, further, that Jesus Christ now rules and reigns over that same world and calls us to live as his disciples—that knowledge is as important for our lives as true north is for the sailor. Under Jesus' guidance, as his students, we may learn not only how to care for the created order, but how to care for our fellow human beings, who are made in the divine image and fashioned for God's purposes.

Jesus, you are Lord over all creation. Teach me and help me to care for this earth, to enjoy its beauty. But also help me care for my fellow human beings, loving them as neighbors who are called to learn from you. Amen.

6. REST: JUST A GOD THING?

The heavens and the earth and all who live in them were
completed. On the sixth day God completed all the work that he
had done, and on the seventh day God rested from all the work
that he had done. God blessed the seventh day and made it holy,
because on it God rested from all the work of creation.
This is the account of the heavens and the earth when they
were created. (Genesis 2:1-4a)

The bulk of my ministry has been dedicated to children, teenagers, and their families. I have noticed this: all of them are busy.
Yet in the Book of Genesis, the first Creation account concludes
with a seventh day when God blessed, sanctified, and rested.

Dan Allender rightly observes, "Few people are willing to enter
the Sabbath and sanctify it, to make it holy, because a full day of
delight and joy is more than most people can bear in a lifetime, let
alone a week."[3] Few of us are willing to practice Sabbath intentionally, to rest from our jobs, sporting activities, extracurriculars,
clubs, and calendar commitments. The creator of the heavens and
the earth may rest, but we do not.

The consequences of our busyness are plain to see. We are worn
out, tired, cranky, and drained. We lack joy and life. But God says,
"Here, let me show you how to live: work, yes, but make time for

rest. Join me in Sabbath. Be with me, be a part of the sanctification of time. See life as a gift; receive life from me."

As you have thought carefully about the Creation story in Genesis 1:1–2:4a, have you come to appreciate more deeply the world God made? Has this story awakened a desire to know God more fully, to serve God more faithfully, and to share God with others? Has the conclusion of this story challenged your rhythms of life, causing you to think more carefully about rest?

May it be so. In a world addicted to activity, slow down. Practice Sabbath. Seek the Lord. Revel in creation. And praise God.

God, you are my Sabbath. May I find rest in you. As you refrained from work and activity on the Sabbath day, blessed that day, and made it holy, may I make space in my life to do the same. Amen.

7. LIVING THE STORY

The stories of Scripture were told not just for information, but for transformation. It is possible to know the Bible cover to cover, but if it has not changed your life—forming, shaping, and reshaping your heart and habits in the image of Jesus Christ—then you may be missing the point.

If you are reading these devotions as a family, use the ideas and activities in the Small Talk children's handout for this week. If you are reading the devotions alone, as a couple, or in a small group, you are invited to take up two practices with Genesis 1:1–2:4a in mind: creation awareness and Sabbath. These practices will challenge you and enable you to grow as a follower of Christ. They will create space where God can transform you, speak to you, guide you, and teach you, by the power of the Holy Spirit.

Creation Awareness

In Genesis 1, God called reality into existence. God said, and it was so. Light and darkness, the sky and bodies of water, the earth, vegetation, sun, moon, and stars, fish of the sea, birds of the air, wildlife, and finally human beings—all were created with words: "Let there be."

Often, we become busy and preoccupied with life, so much so that we do not take time to slow down and notice the world around us. This week, intentionally practice creation awareness. Notice all that God has made. Arrive at scheduled meetings five minutes early and notice your surroundings. Go on a walk with a friend or family member and take note of what you see. All the while, ask God to speak to you through what you observe. In the margin of this book, or in a journal, make some notes about what you hear, what you sense, and what you perceive.

Sabbath

In Genesis 2:1-4a, we read that God rested on the seventh day. How often do you rest? How often do you silence your cell phone or turn it off? How often do you shut down your computer, refrain from using Facebook and Twitter, or look beyond time-consuming news sites? Do you practice Sabbath?

This week, plan to practice Sabbath. Avoid making lists and appointments. Play a game or take a walk outside. Break from your normal routines. Sleep in. Resist the impulse to do. Just be. And watch for signs of God's love for you, apart from what you accomplish. In the margin of this book, or in a journal, make notes about what you hear, what you sense, what you perceive.

Week Two
THE FALL

Genesis 2:4b–3:24

8. DID GOD'S HANDS GET MUDDY?

[T]he LORD God formed the human from the topsoil of the fertile land and blew life's breath into his nostrils. The human came to life. The LORD God planted a garden in Eden in the east and put there the human he had formed. (Genesis 2:7-8)

"Did God's hands get muddy?"

The youngest among us might ask such a question. Don't dismiss it too quickly. The writer of Genesis describes a creative act in which God's hands were plunged into the soil and a human being was crafted, as a child might craft a sand castle. The breath of life was given, mouth to nose, and the human being "came to life." Then God lovingly took the human being to a garden that had been planted in Eden in the east, and gave the human being a place to live.

In this story, God is intimate, close, loving. God is involved. So, did God's hands get muddy? And do they?

The writer of Genesis reminds us that life is fleeting and we are fragile, little more than dirt. Yet, it is God who formed us and gave us life, who brought us into being, who placed us in time and space at this particular moment (Psalm 139; Acts 17). Hold these two truths together: life is short, yet immensely valuable. The God described in Genesis 2, who imparted life to a human being formed from dust, continues to get muddy. That short, transient life of yours is the very place where the eternal God breathes life.

Do you sense the loving care of your creator? Think carefully concerning your life: Where do you see God at work, forming, shaping, and crafting your character, renovating your heart and injecting life? Give thanks.

Where do you see God caring for you, providing you with friends, a community, family, a place to live? Give thanks.

God is at work, with muddy hands and life-giving breath. Trust God's handiwork, and give thanks.

Heavenly God, I trust that you are at work in my life, forming and shaping and giving life. Just as we see you forming the human being from dirt, you are molding the raw material of my being, making me into something that brings you great pleasure. Help me to trust you and give thanks. Amen.

9. CREATED FOR COMMUNITY

*Then the LORD God said, "It's not good that the human is alone.
I will make him a helper that is perfect for him." ... So the LORD
God put the human into a deep and heavy sleep, and took one of
his ribs and closed up the flesh over it. With the rib taken from
the human, the LORD God fashioned a woman and brought her to
the human being. The human said, "This one finally is bone from
my bones and flesh from my flesh. She will be called a woman
because from a man she was taken." This is the reason that a man
leaves his father and mother and embraces his wife, and they
become one flesh. The two of them were naked, the man and his
wife, but they weren't embarrassed. (Genesis 2:18; 21-25)*

As a fifth grader, I was unsure if I was liked. While camping
with my class, I slipped away from a game of baseball to the shore
of a nearby lake, and prayed this prayer: "Lord, if I have friends,
can you show me a sign?"

Moments later, Matt took a seat next to me and asked what
I was thinking about. Less than a minute after that, every other
student in my class had gathered nearby, sitting on the shoreline,
looking out on the water. God answered that prayer.

Our reading today teaches us a great deal. Before human beings
experienced broken fellowship with God in the Genesis story, God
saw that "it is not good that the human is alone." God then made a

helper, a woman, "perfect" for the human being. The woman was crafted from a rib taken from the man's side. The man rejoiced when he saw what God had done, and they were together in perfect togetherness.

We are made for relationships. We desire the loving companionship of others, because we literally were made for it. That longing is satisfied first through a relationship with God, and second through a relationship with our neighbor. Both are essential.

Think about your relationships. If you are in need of friendship, spend time with others. Think of those who may be lonely. Reach out; be a companion sent by God.

Lord God, I am made for relationship. May I love you, and may I love my neighbor. Amen.

10. Daring, Defiance, Disaster

*The snake was the most intelligent of all the wild animals that
the Lord God had made. He said to the woman, "Did God really
say that you shouldn't eat from any tree in the garden?" The
woman said to the snake, "We may eat the fruit of the garden's
trees but not the fruit of the tree in the middle of the garden. God
said, 'Don't eat from it, and don't touch it, or you will die.'"*
(Genesis 3:1-3)

In the film *Finding Nemo*, Marlin, a clown fish, is upset. His
son, Nemo, has headed to the edge of the reef on his first day of
school. Marlin has told his son repeatedly to avoid risk and stay
safe. He has tried to keep his son from harm. But Nemo's class-
mates quickly put him in danger. Together, Nemo and his three
friends brave the open water beyond the reef, daring one another
to swim farther away from the safety of the coral.

Marlin, worried about what may take place while Nemo is
out of his sight, follows the class to the reef. He finds Nemo and
pulls him back from peril. Then, while Marlin talks to the teacher,
Nemo swims out in the open water, daring to touch a boat in the
distance despite a weak fin. Marlin tells him to stop, but Nemo
defies him. And disaster ensues.

Genesis 3 tells a similar story. The woman is faced with temptation, and she is deceived. She is tempted by the serpent to disobey

God and does something she knows is wrong. She wants what the serpent has promised. Remaining obedient to God's command no longer seems best. And disaster ensues.

Oftentimes, we are tempted. The forbidden becomes appealing. A voice whispers, "Did God really say . . . ?" And we give in.

Resist temptation. Listen to what God has commanded. Pray for the wisdom to know good from evil and for the strength to choose the good.

Holy Spirit, fill me with wisdom and strength, that I may obey God's commands. Keep me from temptation, and drive the evil one from my presence. May I live a life that is pleasing to you. Amen.

11. RESOURCES FOR RESISTING

Then the Spirit led Jesus up into the wilderness so that the devil might tempt him. After Jesus had fasted for forty days and forty nights, he was starving. The tempter came to him and said, "Since you are God's Son, command these stones to become bread." (Matthew 4:1-3)

How do we resist temptation? One way is to learn the stories of the Bible and memorize the words of Scripture.

Pastor Joshua Choonmin Kang writes, "When we meditate deeply on the words of Scripture, we begin to bear fruit. But before we can meditate scripturally, we must have a scriptural treasure in our heart. The words of Scripture must be safely deposited in the vaults and chambers of our innermost heart."[4]

In Matthew 4, Jesus was tempted three times, and each time he quoted from the Book of Deuteronomy. Jesus had heeded the words of the psalmist: "Thy word have I hid in mine heart, that I might not sin against thee" (Psalm 119:11 KJV).

The story of Jesus' temptation is striking, because it resembles the story of Eve's temptation in Genesis 3. But Jesus' story differs in one important respect: he resisted the temptation.

Jesus sought above all to obey the call that God had placed upon his life. He was singularly focused on one thing: the mission

God had sent him to accomplish. His utmost desire was clear: living a life that was pleasing to the Lord.

God has provided you with all the resources you need to do likewise. The fuel that runs the engine is called grace. The good news about grace is this: it never runs out.

Do you find yourself tempted? Trust God. Call on God's name. Bring the words of God's story, given in the Bible, readily to mind. If you fail? Repent, and begin again. Christ's grace is sufficient. Learn your lesson, admit your failure, lean on God, seek the will of the Lord, and do it.

Jesus Christ, Son of God, have mercy on me, a sinner. Help me to memorize the words of Scripture, to familiarize myself with the story of the Bible, and to live faithfully according to what I find. May I trust in your grace to perform your will. You are my strength and my righteousness; I place my hope in you. Amen.

12. NOTICING RESTORATION

The LORD God made the man and his wife leather clothes and dressed them. (Genesis 3:21)

In 2004, Victoria Ruvolo was the victim of a teenage prank. Cruising down the roadway, a young man leaned out the window of his vehicle with a large, frozen turkey and tossed it into the windshield of Ruvolo's oncoming car.

A month later, she woke up in a hospital bed. She underwent countless surgeries, an induced coma, and extensive rehabilitation.

Later, the teenager went to trial. His sentence: six months in jail and five years probation. After sentencing, Ruvolo said, "I told him 'Just do something good with your life.' And then I hugged him."[5]

When we read the story of Genesis 3, we often note the sly words of the serpent, the taking of the forbidden fruit, the discord that resulted, and the proclamation of God that followed. We quake as God metes out punishment. But often we overlook grace.

God gave the man and woman one prohibition in the garden: do not eat the fruit of one tree. All the other trees were available. But the man and the woman were tempted, and they fell prey. Theologians have speculated regarding what this story means for all of humanity. Some arguments are more convincing than others.

But the focus is most often placed on the consequences of disobedience, rather than the restoration that follows.

The story of Victoria Ruvolo is one of forgiveness and restoration. She could have demanded a stricter sentence for the young prankster; instead, she encouraged leniency.

When the man and woman took and ate from the forbidden tree, God rightly dispensed consequences. But then God went about the work of restoration. A sacrifice was given. The clothes that the man and the woman had made from fig leaves were discarded and replaced with garments made of leather. Grace began to take effect, foreshadowing a greater sacrifice—and a greater restoration—that was to come in Christ.

What is remarkable about the story of Victoria Ruvolo is the restoration. Remarkable, too, is the restoration in the story of Genesis 3. Despite our failings, God acts to redeem us.

Holy God, you are the great restoration artist. When my life is broken to pieces, you put me back together. When I sin against you, you extend grace. Thank you, thank you, thank you! Amen.

13. GRACE IS GREATER THAN ...

*The gift isn't like the consequences of one person's sin. The
judgment that came from one person's sin led to punishment, but
the free gift that came out of many failures led to the verdict of
acquittal. If death ruled because of one person's failure, those
who receive the multiplied grace and the gift of righteousness
will even more certainly rule in life through the one person
Jesus Christ. (Romans 5:16-17)*

Grace is God's love and forgiveness, given to us even though
we don't deserve it. It's the "free gift" in today's Scripture.

Thinking about that Scripture, a pastor friend of mine captured
its truth by borrowing a mathematical concept called an inequal-
ity. His expression: "Grace > _____."[6] Put anything in the blank.
Sorrow. Anger. Revenge. Heartache. Grief. Sin. Grace is bigger.
Grace is superior. Grace outweighs it.

Grace can overcome it. Grace can get you through it, because
grace finds its source in the revelatory, self-giving, and sacrificial
life of Jesus Christ.

Read in isolation, the story of the man and woman eating the
forbidden fruit appears to us as a tragic tale of human failing.
And indeed, that view is true. But read within the context of the
whole of Scripture, the story takes on a deeper significance. In
the Book of Romans, Paul looks back to this narrative and tells us

something of Christ and the new work that God has brought about through him.

Adam failed; there was consequence. Christ succeeded; there is abundance. Grace is greater than sin. The result should be a heart overflowing with thanksgiving to God. Think of how much you have been given! God loves you. God has overcome your sin. God has extended to you the gift of eternal life.

The English poet and Anglican priest George Herbert captured the idea in this way: "Thou that hast given so much to me, / Give one thing more—a grateful heart.…"[7]

How do you express thanks for the gift of life that Christ has given you?

Covenant God, you have brought about the redemption of all people through your son, Jesus Christ. Where Adam's action brought judgment, you have brought grace. You have given us the hope of eternal life; we are made right with you through Christ. May we trust in your goodness. May we see that you have accomplished your purposes. And by faith, may we discover that you are truly good. Amen.

14. Living the Story

If you are reading these devotions as a family, use the ideas and activities in the Small Talk children's handout for this week. If you are reading the devotions by yourself, as a couple, or in a small group, you are invited to take up two practices: hospitality and the *examen*. These practices will challenge you and enable you to grow as a follower of Christ. They will create space where God can transform you, speak to you, guide you, and teach you, by the power of the Holy Spirit.

Hospitality

"It's not good that the human is alone." We read these words in Genesis, and we know them to be true. We are made for community.

This week, practice hospitality. Invite a friend to coffee or lunch. Make it your treat. Keep the focus of conversation on the other person, if possible, but don't decline to answer if they wish to ask you questions. Ask about family, work, school, and what the person has done for fun. Ask about dreams and aspirations— vacations or life goals. Listen deeply. Receive your guest as you would Christ.

The *Examen*

In a journal or on a computer, write and reflect on your most common failings. Where do you consistently struggle to live faithfully as a disciple of Jesus? Based on your most common struggles, make a list of three to five questions to evaluate how and when you fail, and how you might better serve Christ in the future.

For example, you may find you do not treat everyone equally as a creation of God. Ask yourself at the conclusion of each day, "Have I treated each person I encountered with the dignity deserved by one made in the image of God? If yes, where did God assist me? If no, how might I act differently tomorrow?"

Regular engagement with the *examen* will help you to focus on specific areas of growth and will help maintain an ongoing conversation with God regarding the areas most in need of attention. The early Methodist societies would routinely ask the question, "How is it with your soul?" Make it a practice this week to reflect on your soul, either on your own or in conversation with a trusted friend.

Week Three
THE FLOOD

Genesis 6:5–9:17

15. WE MATTER

But as for Noah, the LORD approved of him. (Genesis 6:8)

My friend Joe works with high school students. He finds that his greatest challenge is helping adolescents experience approval, acceptance, and love. Teenagers want to belong. They want to know that someone, somewhere validates their existence and delights in their lives. They want to know that they matter.

Though the story of Noah and the Great Flood is about judgment, it is also about redemption, approval, acceptance, and hope. God is grieved by the wickedness of people but does not completely abandon the human project. Noah is deemed righteous by God; God approves of his life. God then works to preserve Noah and a remnant of the creation. God's judgment rightly gives us reason to measure the consequences of our wrongdoing. But Noah's redemption gives us reason to measure God's concern for what has been made.

Human beings have worth. We matter. And divine approval is the ultimate validation of this reality. The Lord approved of Noah. How do we find approval?

Approval is not ours to win but ours to accept. Jesus Christ, God in the flesh, has come by divine approval on our behalf and dispenses love and acceptance to all of us who place our faith in him.

It is written in Galatians 2:16, "We ourselves believed in Christ Jesus so that we could be made righteous by the faithfulness of Christ and not by the works of the Law—because no one will be made righteous by the works of the Law." And again in Galatians 2:19b-20, "I have been crucified with Christ and I no longer live, but Christ lives in me. And the life that I now live in my body, I live by faith, indeed, by the faithfulness of God's Son, who loved me and gave himself for me."

Find approval in Christ. You are more loved than you ever dared hope. Trust in him and in his work.

Lord God Almighty, may I trust in your great love for me. May I give up my striving for approval and acceptance and realize that, in you, I already am. Just as you welcomed Noah as your friend, you welcome me. I am thankful for your friendship. Amen.

16. Agents of Restoration

In God's sight, the earth had become corrupt and was filled with violence. God saw that the earth was corrupt, because all creatures behaved corruptly on the earth. (Genesis 6:11-12)

The stories of the Bible are utterly realistic. The world we live in is burdened by sin and wickedness. Wars are fought unjustly, the poor are neglected, the widows are ignored. Children are hungry, families are broken, and governments are corrupt.

But that is not the whole story. God is working to set things right, and you are invited to be part of the project. Where there is war, you are called to be a peacemaker. Where the poor are neglected, you are called to bring healing. Where widows are ignored, you are called to remember. Feed the hungry, give drink to the thirsty, visit the prisoner, give clothing to the naked. In Christ, you are called to be an agent of restoration, a divine vehicle for the magnificent work of God.

What does that work look like for you at school? At work? In your family? In your church and community?

If you're in school, you may be called to stand up to a bully. You may be called to remain honest in test taking or on homework assignments, when others cut corners. If you're at work, you may need to challenge your coworkers to integrity in transactions and then to model that course of action. If you are a parent, you may be called to make difficult decisions in loving and protecting your children.

God calls us to a thousand small actions to perform in God's name. Are you listening to the quiet voice of the Holy Spirit? Are you taking part in the healing work of Almighty God?

You may wonder where to start. Begin with prayer: "Lord, help me to see as you see and to act as you would have me act."

God, the Judge, you look upon the earth and see where there is discord and where there is wholeness. Just as in the days of Noah, corruption, wickedness, and violence remain upon the earth. But we know that you have struck a decisive blow to injustice in the person of Jesus Christ, and you have called us to be part of your redeeming work. Help us to be agents of your healing, your hope, and your restoration. Amen.

17. WHO DO YOU FOLLOW?

Make your ways known to me, LORD; teach me your paths.
Lead me in your truth—teach it to me—because you are the
God who saves me. I put my hope in you all day long. LORD,
remember your compassion and faithful love—they are forever!
But don't remember the sins of my youth or my wrongdoing.
Remember me only according to your faithful love for the sake
of your goodness, LORD. (Psalm 25:4-7)

I grew up playing sports. The game I have come to love most is basketball. There have been many coaches who have helped me understand the game and improve in skill, and because of their efforts I experience joy each time I step on the court.

I believe that in order for people to improve or master their particular love—sports or otherwise—they will need help. They will need a teacher, a coach, or a mentor who shows them how it is done.

It's true of Christian spiritual life, too. We need to be taught God's ways, God's path, and God's truth. Why? The psalmist says "because you are the God who saves me." Noah knew that it was true. In Genesis 6–7, he built the ark as God commanded, while his neighbors paid no attention. Noah trusted God.

In John 14:6a, Jesus declared, "I am the way, the truth, and the life." For Christians, Jesus is our teacher and mentor. God's way of "making known" our way of life is not simply to tell, but to show. When we look to Jesus, we not only hear his words, but we see his actions. If we pattern our lives after his, Jesus promises he will teach us.

In Jesus Christ, we are called to trust God and to live in an interactive relationship with God. How are you actively learning to live as Jesus' disciple?

Jesus Christ, my teacher, I place my life at your feet. I want to be your student. Teach me to obey all that you have commanded. Help me to follow the pattern of your perfect life. Remake me in your image, so that when others look at me, they will see you. I trust in you, knowing that you love me beyond measure. Amen.

18. THE PROMISE-KEEPING GOD

Noah built an altar to the LORD. He took some of the clean large animals and some of the clean birds, and placed entirely burned offerings on the altar. The LORD smelled the pleasing scent, and the LORD thought to himself, I will not curse the fertile land anymore because of human beings since the ideas of the human mind are evil from their youth. I will never again destroy every living thing as I have done. As long as the earth exists, seedtime and harvest, cold and hot, summer and autumn, day and night will not cease. (Genesis 8:20-22)

"Cross my heart, and hope to die." With those words, I have sealed many promises. I have made promises to siblings, to my wife, to my daughter, and to friends.

I know what it is like to make promises, what it is like to keep them, and what it is like to break them. Making them means I must be responsible, keeping them shows that I am faithful to my word, and breaking them gets me in trouble.

Throughout the Bible, God is described as a God who makes and keeps promises, who is sure to follow through.

An old hymn declares, "Standing on the promises that cannot fail, / when the howling storms of doubt and fear assail, / by the living Word of God I shall prevail, / standing on the promises of

45

God."[8] What are the promises of Scripture that you know well, that you claim each day, and that strengthen you as you follow Jesus?

Take a moment today to recall the promises God makes in Scripture. Ask a friend, family member, or pastor to help expand your list. During the quiet moments of your day, perhaps following lunch or before bed, review what you have written. Place your faith in the promise-keeping God.

God who keeps promises, I call on your name. You have made a covenant with human beings, and in Jesus Christ I trust you have been faithful to that covenant. You are working to make this world new, not to destroy it. Like Noah, may I make a sacrifice, not of animals but of my life. May what you find there be pleasing to you, and may you include me in your work to keep promises to this world. Amen.

19. The Sign of a Promise

God said, "This is the symbol of the covenant that I am drawing up between me and you and every living thing with you, on behalf of every future generation. I have placed my bow in the clouds; it will be the symbol of the covenant between me and the earth." (Genesis 9:12-13)

Have you ever seen a sign carved in the trunk of a tree? Perhaps it was a heart with initials inside, a symbol left behind to declare that once, in this place, two lovers pledged their dedication to one another. Anyone passing by could see it and ponder. As for the lovers, for years to come it would remind them of the commitment that once was, and might still be.

In the story of Noah, God placed a rainbow in the clouds as a sign of his covenant following the Great Flood. When human beings see it, they are to remember its meaning and recall the promise God made, not only to Noah but to the generations that would follow. It was a sign meant to endure forever.

The rainbow is not the only symbol we associate with God's promises. The cross is another, displayed in most churches to remind us of Christ's sacrifice for us. Other symbols often are incorporated into stained glass or other artwork in our church buildings, such as the lamb, the living water, a harp, or bread and a cup of wine.

The signs of God's faithfulness may also be people—a child who was long hoped for, a relative who survived an illness, a grandmother who has prayed for you every day since your birth and has loved you well. God places reminders all around us.

What signs and symbols, like the rainbow, remind you that God is faithful to the promises that have been made? Open your eyes, look around, and give thanks.

God, you walk with me through life, always active, always present. You have revealed yourself to me through events, friends, family, and strangers, as well as through your church. The signs are everywhere. May I remember those moments when you have shown yourself faithful and give thanks to you. Amen.

20. RESCUED THROUGH WATER

*In the past, these spirits were disobedient—when God patiently
waited during the time of Noah. Noah built an ark in which a
few (that is, eight) lives were rescued through water. Baptism
is like that. It saves you now—not because it removes dirt from
your body but because it is the mark of a good conscience
toward God. Your salvation comes through the resurrection of
Jesus Christ, who is at God's right side. Now that he has gone
into heaven, he rules over all angels, authorities, and powers.*
(1 Peter 3:20-22)

While driving, if you face an intersection marked by a red octa-
gon with a giant four-letter word printed in white letters, what do
you do? *Stop!*

Signs and symbols dot the landscape of our everyday experience. The church has an important symbol we often celebrate:
baptism.

Symbols teach and instruct us. What do the waters of baptism
teach?

Baptism is a sign of God's covenant love for us. The water is an
outward and visible sign of an inward and invisible reality: God, in
Christ, has set us right. The early Christians saw something of the
Noah story in their experience of Jesus. As in the story of Noah,
God has rescued us, this time not from a flood but from the power

of sin. Baptism is a symbol of our salvation, which, as we read in today's Scripture, "comes though the resurrection of Jesus Christ." Baptism also reminds us of the authority of Christ, the one above the symbol itself.

Baptism is for the young and old. Have you been baptized? If not, why delay? If so, do you remember your baptism? Even if you were a small infant, you likely have heard stories of that day. In conversation, tell the story.

If you do not remember or do not know the details, don't worry. We do not remember every instance in which grace pounced upon us without permission. God was at work. Trust in that.

Lord Jesus, may I remember my baptism. May I remember that you have placed a claim on me and, through the witness of your church, I have been buried with you, yet raised to walk in newness of life. You have saved and redeemed me, just as you did Noah. May I be a good steward of the life you have given to me, faithful to you in all you command. Strengthen me for the task. Amen.

21. Living the Story

If you are reading these devotions as a family, use the ideas and activities in the Small Talk children's handout for this week. If you are reading the devotions alone, as a couple, or in a small group, you are invited to take up two practices: memorizing Scripture and making an art project called a covenant collage. These practices will challenge you and enable you to grow as a follower of Christ. They will create space where God can transform you, speak to you, guide you, and teach you, by the power of the Holy Spirit.

Memorizing Scripture

This practice may seem old-fashioned, but it can be extremely valuable. In the story of Noah, God makes a covenant with human beings after the Great Flood. The words of the covenant serve as a reminder of God's faithfulness and tell us something of God's character. Other verses of Scripture capture aspects of God's character as well, or expectations that God has for human beings. Memorizing this information helps us to make better decisions, and also enables us to meditate on who God is as we move through each day, strengthening our relationship with God.

Choose three to five verses of Scripture and write them down on separate note cards. You may wish to put the verse on one side and the reference on the opposite side. Carry these with you, and when you have a few free moments, read the words and commit them to your heart.

A Covenant Collage

What are the signs and symbols you readily associate with God's love and faithfulness?

In the story of Noah, a rainbow reminds people of God's covenant. For me, pictures of my family or objects given to me by loved ones remind me of God's love. I wear a cross around my neck each day as another reminder of my calling in Christ.

This week, obtain a large piece of paper, magazines, or other materials and create a covenant collage. Include in your collage symbols of God's faithfulness to you, and offer God thanks as you bring these things to mind. You may also wish to include symbols that remind you of the life God has called you to live, not only symbols of what you have received. When you're finished, put the collage somewhere you will see it on a regular basis.

FATHER ABRAHAM

Genesis 12:1-3; 15:1-6; 22:1-19

22. THE COST AND THE BLESSING

The LORD said to Abram, "Leave your land, your family, and your father's household for the land that I will show you. I will make of you a great nation and will bless you. I will make your name respected, and you will be a blessing. I will bless those who bless you, those who curse you I will curse; all the families of earth will be blessed because of you." (Genesis 12:1-3)

Faithfulness to God the Father, Son, and Holy Spirit often leads us to places we do not expect and asks of us great sacrifice. Abram, in Genesis 12, is given a great promise. But first, he is asked to give up everything. We like to focus our attention on the words, "I will make..." and "I will bless...," but God's call begins with "Leave."

Discipleship to Jesus Christ is always costly. Like Abram, we must be prepared to leave land, family, and inheritance to claim the life God has for us. We recognize that this is no small price, but the gain far exceeds what we leave behind. Exactly what we are asked to give up will vary from one person to the next, depending on our social context and background. But it will be a kind of death—a leaving behind of one life for another. As the German pastor and theologian Dietrich Bonhoeffer wrote, "When Christ calls a man, he bids him come and die."[9]

Abram was promised a destination, a people, and a blessing. That promise has been fulfilled in Jesus Christ, and we share as recipients of the blessing. Our destination: the kingdom of heaven, present wherever those who call on Jesus are found. Our people: the church, partnering with God to bring about the restoration of all things. Our blessing: a relationship with God, by virtue of faith in Jesus Christ.

What does it mean for us to be brought into the story of Abram? What has God asked us to leave behind? And what work have we been called to, that we might be a blessing and that all the nations of the earth might be blessed by God through us?

Lord, may my faith be like that of Abram, who set aside all he knew to go on a journey with you. May I live in to the promises you made to him, because you have made me an heir through Christ. In his name. Amen.

23. Living an Incredible Story

Then he brought Abram outside and said, "Look up at the sky and count the stars if you think you can count them." He continued, "This is how many children you will have." Abram trusted the LORD, and the LORD recognized Abram's high moral character.
(Genesis 15:5-6)

Have you ever been confronted with something you found inconceivable, something too amazing to believe?

We like fantastic stories that stretch our imaginations and expand our creative horizons. We are drawn to these stories because they speak to us of possibilities, of the chance to see and experience things we have not encountered before.

This is one of those stories.

Abram, now a very old man, was talking with God. God had promised him a large family, but Abram did not yet have a rightful heir. His wife, Sarai, was also in old age and beyond childbearing years. Yet God kept reminding Abram of the promise, and, in spite of a few bumps along the way, Abram kept trusting God to deliver on that promise.

Sometime in your own life, you may find yourself in Abram's shoes, trusting God to deliver on a promise. God may call on you to place your trust in a future you cannot see. It won't be until you come out the other side, until the story has reached its climax and resolution, that you realize your story has become something too amazing to believe.

Do you think Abram, while talking with God, ever said to himself, "Oh, my, this ordinary life I'm living, waiting for a son, will one day be discussed by people more numerous than the stars in the sky"? Not likely. Abram simply took the next step.

And so, too, it is with us. God is calling you to trust in purposes you cannot fully see or understand, and to simply take the next step. Keep track of the story, keep an eye out for God, and when the plot turns, be ready to experience wonder, awe, and even worship.

Then you will have a story to tell.

God of Abram, you have been faithful. What Abram could not begin to fathom has come into being: I am your child, by virtue of the covenant you made with Abram and his family. What a miracle! May I have faith in you, as Abram had faith in you, and may you see fit to credit it to me as righteousness. Amen.

24. The Surprise Invitation

So Abraham is our father in the eyes of God in whom he had faith, the God who gives life to the dead and calls things that don't exist into existence. (Romans 4:17b)

Have you ever received a surprise invitation?

John Wesley is remembered as a leading figure in the Methodist revival in England. Though he had known of Christ his entire life, Wesley famously wrote in his journal of a transforming encounter he had with Christ, dated May 24, 1738: "In the evening, I went very unwillingly to a society in Aldersgate Street. . . . About a quarter before nine . . . I felt my heart strangely warmed. I felt I did trust Christ, Christ alone for my salvation; and an assurance was given me that he had taken away my sins, even mine, and saved me from the law of sin and death."[10]

John Wesley experienced the grace of Jesus Christ, and he was surprised. He was made part of the story of Abraham. He was invited. He accepted. You're invited, too.

You matter to God. Through Jesus Christ, God has brought you into a new family, the family of Abram, who became known as Abraham. In the fourth century, an interpreter of Scripture known as Ambrosiaster wrote concerning today's verse, "In order to teach that there is one God for all, Paul tells the Gentiles that Abraham believed in God himself and was justified in his sight."[11]

In the story of Abraham, God was doing a new thing. God began with a promise: "I will make of you a great nation and will bless you... you will be a blessing... all the families of earth will be blessed because of you" (Genesis 12:1-3). When Paul and other Christian interpreters read those texts and listened to Jesus' earliest disciples, they concluded God had fulfilled that promise in Jesus Christ, "the descendant" of Abraham (Galatians 3:16). What a surprise!

You are invited to be part of what God began with Abraham. Surprised? Like Abraham, have faith. Trust God, and live as a member of God's family.

God, you began a wonderful work in Abraham and continued it in Jesus Christ. May I take my place in the family of faith. Amen.

25. THE GREAT TEST

After these events, God tested Abraham and said to him, "Abraham!" Abraham answered, "I'm here." God said, "Take your son, your only son whom you love, Isaac, and go to the land of Moriah. Offer him up as an entirely burned offering there on one of the mountains that I will show you." (Genesis 22:1-2)

We are all familiar with tests. Teachers use tests to measure knowledge. Debate teams face tests when confronting opponents in tournament. Our character can be tested when we are faced with a difficult choice.

But this? The story of Abraham describes a test surpassing all tests. God told Abraham to take his son, "your only son whom you love," and to prepare him for sacrifice. Abraham faced the test and set off to do as God had commanded.

The Danish philosopher Søren Kierkegaard found Abraham's actions beyond explanation, saying that Abraham was a true "knight of faith," one who obeyed God even when called to do something beyond rationality.[12] Abraham's faith was radical and extreme, raising questions about the very nature of God. Could such a God be trusted? Abraham believed so.

How about you? Can you trust the God who tested Abraham?

God may call you to something radical, something having the appearance of risk. You may be called to speak out against injustice or give up financial gain to serve the poor. You may be called to befriend outsiders who are sneered at by your peers. You may be called to stand up to a bully, even when it hurts.

You may be called to make as much money as you can, only to give it away. You may be called to the ministry, or to be a mother. When God speaks, it may be a test of faith. Will you listen? If you hear, will you obey? Can this God be trusted?

Abraham believed so. So do I. Have faith.

God of Abraham, give me a radical faith. Enable me to trust you when tested. Amen.

26. A Capable Captain

On the third day, Abraham looked up and saw the place at a distance. Abraham said to his servants, "Stay here with the donkey. The boy and I will walk up there, worship, and then come back to you." (Genesis 22:4-5)

Christians have long read the story of Abraham and Isaac as one of great faith, as well as a story that challenges our trust in the good purposes of God. The obedience we see modeled by Abraham makes our own confidence in God look puny. Few will readily say, "My faith is as great as Abraham's."

Charles Haddon Spurgeon, the great Baptist preacher, once told a story to illustrate the obedience of faith and the confidence faith should inspire. Spurgeon began, "The ship is on fire; the bales of cotton are pouring forth a black, horrible smoke; passengers and crew are in extreme danger, but a capable captain is in command, and he says to those around him, 'If you will behave yourselves, I think I shall be able to effect the escape of you all.'" The captain gives commands, and those on board "believe his orders to be wise, and so they keep them." The result is safety for all passengers and crew, to the great relief of all.

Spurgeon then challenged the faith of his hearers: "Obedience is the necessary outcome of true and real faith, and there is no trust where there is no obedience....The faith which saves is a faith which obeys."[13]

Abraham believed God, as Spurgeon's crew believed their captain. God had been revealed to Abraham as a God who could be trusted. Abraham trusted God when told to leave behind family, land, and inheritance. Abraham, even in old age, trusted God when told he would have a son. Abraham's obedience proved his trust. His words reveal his confidence in God while facing this test: Abraham told his servants that after they had ascended the mountain and worshiped, they would return, "the boy and I."

Each day you will have opportunities to demonstrate your faith through obedience. What has God called you to do at school, at home, or at work that is a challenge for you? Ask God for help, and trust in the Holy Spirit. God is with you.

Lord Jesus, may I show my faith by my obedience. Amen.

27. THE GREATER TEST

They arrived at the place God had described to him. Abraham built an altar there and arranged the wood on it. He tied up his son Isaac and laid him on the altar on top of the wood. Then Abraham stretched out his hand and took the knife to kill his son as a sacrifice. But the LORD's messenger called out to Abraham from heaven, "Abraham? Abraham?" Abraham said, "I'm here." (Genesis 22:9-11)

For Christians, the story of Abraham and Isaac provides much to ponder. The details sound familiar. A father takes a son to sacrifice. The son is placed upon wood to be killed. Yet where God stopped Abraham before Isaac died, God did not stop the death of Jesus Christ. Christ went to Calvary, obedient to the will of the Father. He placed his body upon the wood of the cross as an act of divine love for humankind.

As Abraham was given a ram as a substitute for his son, so we, too, are provided a substitute. Jesus stands in our place upon the cross. As 1 Peter 2:24 says, "He carried in his own body on the cross the sins we committed. He did this so that we might live in righteousness, having nothing to do with sin. By his wounds you were healed."

The story of Abraham and Isaac stands on its own, but for Christians it points beyond that. The cross of Christ casts a long shadow, showing that where Abraham was tested, Jesus underwent and passed a greater test for us.

Can you see it? A glimpse of that greater test will melt your heart and move you to action. As you face tests, serve God today out of the abundance of God's love for all of us, demonstrated in Jesus Christ.

Lord God, grant me the grace to possess a faith like Abraham's— attentive to your voice, trusting you when tested, and true to the end. Help me to see in the story of Abraham the story of Jesus Christ, and may that, too, inspire my faith. Amen.

28. LIVING THE STORY

If you are reading these devotions as a family, use the ideas and activities in the Small Talk children's handout for this week. If you are reading the devotions alone, as a couple, or in a small group, you are invited to take up two practices: counting your blessings and silence. These practices will challenge you and enable you to grow as a follower of Christ. They will create space where God can transform you, speak to you, guide you, and teach you, by the power of the Holy Spirit.

Counting Your Blessings

In the story of Abraham, God promised to bless him so that Abraham might be a blessing. Using a journal or a blank piece of paper, list some of the ways you have been blessed. Think of things both great and small. You may think of your church as a great blessing; ice cream may be something small.

Counting our blessings helps us to notice the many ways God is faithful to us in our daily lives. We often focus on the negative and as a result become burdened and weary, even when good things are taking place around us. By counting our blessings, we bring our lives back into focus. We are better able to see our hardships and struggles in light of God's mercy. The result may be joy, thanksgiving, and a greater sense of peace.

Silence

Turn off your computer and cell phone and find a time and place to be silent. It may be on a walk in a quiet park or in your room, seated in your favorite chair. In the silence of the night, Abraham was able to hear God's voice calling him, asking him to look up at the stars and to imagine what God intended to do through him. Our attention, our full presence, and a posture of listening are needed so that God can teach us and lead us.

Be still, and listen for God's quiet voice. Examine your own life, and turn what you discover over to God's merciful care. Draw near to God.

Week Five
TEN WORDS

Exodus 20:1-17

29. NONE BEFORE ME

Then God spoke all these words: I am the LORD your God who brought you out of Egypt, out of the house of slavery. You must have no other gods before me. (Exodus 20:1-3)

Dallas Willard, a professor of philosophy at the University of Southern California, stated plainly, "The Ten Commandments... are God's best information on how to lead a basically decent human existence."[14] Yet how many of us can name those commandments? How many of us strive to follow them?

These "Ten Words" are of great importance. The first commandment has a distinction. It contains a declaration of who God is. It is not so much a rule as it is a reminder. God delivered the people of Israel from Egypt, and out of slavery. God says, "I'm first. The rest of what I'm about to tell you follows from who I am and from my relationship to you."

For Israel, and for us, our problems begin when we forget who God is and what our relationship to God is like. We run after "other gods" and worship them instead of the true God, the God who has been with us through thick and thin.

We trade the God of love for the god of popularity. We trade the God who saves for the god of power. We trade the God who delivers us for the god of worldly success. Without realizing it, we soon find ourselves in a "house of slavery," having chosen our own chains.

Examine your heart. Is God first? Do you worship God above all other gods? Worship of the true God puts our pursuit of success, popularity, and beauty in their proper place.

Give your life to the God who first loved you. God will lead you to a better land.

God who delivers me, lead me into your company so that I might worship you. May I then worship you, you alone, leaving "other gods" behind. Amen.

30. Casting Down Idols

Do not make an idol for yourself—no form whatsoever—of anything in the sky above or on the earth below or in the waters under the earth. Do not bow down to them or worship them, because I, the LORD your God, am a passionate God.
(Exodus 20:4-5a)

The second commandment speaks in terms that are strange to us. Who can relate to what it asks? "Do not make an idol," it says. What does this mean?

Today, very few of us craft statues to display in our homes, calling them gods. We do not go to a place of worship and bow down before an object of devotion. Do we?

The ancients named their gods and created images that could be seen and touched. Their gods had names. For the Greeks, Zeus was foremost among the gods; for the Romans, Mars was the god of war. The nations surrounding Israel worshiped Baal and Asherah.

Our idols aren't so obvious. We don't often give them names. But we do have them. We worship sports stars, celebrities, and politicians. We might not call them gods, but we idolize them. We also worship our notions of success and beauty. We might not pray to these gods, but some of us make choices revealing that these things have the highest value in our lives.

Timothy J. Keller wrote, "An idol is whatever you look at and say, in your heart of hearts, 'If I have that, then I'll feel my life has meaning, then I'll know I have value, then I'll feel significant and secure.' There are many ways to describe this kind of relationship to something, but perhaps the best one is worship."[15]

The second commandment remains relevant. We may not make little statues, but we do identify certain values or ideals and put them in the place of God. We make sacrifices to these gods, and we worship them. How do we stop?

One way is to identify our inclination to worship things other than God. But that is only a step. We must see that the God revealed in Jesus Christ puts all our desires in their proper place and that God is our ultimate aim.

Examine your heart. Is God first?

God who is worthy of worship, may you take first place in my heart, in my life. In the name of Christ. Amen.

31. The Lord's Wisdom

The Lord's Instruction is perfect, reviving one's very being. The Lord's laws are faithful, making naive people wise. The Lord's regulations are right, gladdening the heart. The Lord's commands are pure, giving light to the eyes. (Psalm 19:7-8)

For several years, I worked as a school bus driver. Laws, regulations, and safety instructions were constant concerns. Not only did we want to ensure that our drivers were aware of the rules enforceable by police officers, we wanted everyone to remain accident free and clear of danger.

Just as the laws, regulations, and safety instructions I received as a school bus driver were meant to help me perform my job better, the Ten Commandments and other instructions found in Scripture are meant to enrich our lives. They are not meant to be a burden, but rather meant to create boundaries that will enable us to flourish. The psalmist in today's Scripture recognizes this. God's instruction is "perfect," "reviving," "faithful," "making...wise," "right," "pure," and "giving light."

Christians believe that, in addition to the Bible, Jesus Christ himself teaches us. We are meant to engage in an interactive relationship with God, one of prayer, action, listening, learning, and transformation. As C. S. Lewis expressed so well, "The real Son of God is at your side. He is beginning to turn you into the same kind of thing as Himself. He is beginning...to 'inject' His kind of life and thought...into you; beginning to turn the tin soldier into a live man."[16]

Growing into the person God has designed you to be requires opening your life to Jesus Christ, as well as to teachers, pastors, friends, and mentors who can help you along the way. Take a moment today to consider two things. First, what parts of the Bible have enriched your life? And second, who has helped you to see and understand the life God is calling you to live? You may wish to write a note, e-mail, or text to that person expressing your thanks.

God, thank you for giving us the gift of the Bible and the commandments found within it. May I be open to the teaching of Jesus and other reliable guides so that I might live more faithfully as your disciple. May I find great joy in your instruction. Amen.

32. MIND THE RULES

Honor your father and your mother so that your life will be long on the fertile land that the LORD your God is giving you. Do not kill. Do not commit adultery. Do not steal. Do not testify falsely against your neighbor. Do not desire your neighbor's house.
(Exodus 20:12-17a)

During my work as a school bus driver, I would post rules at the beginning of each year. I would take time and explain these rules to the students. "Don't make too much noise." "Don't clog the aisle." "Don't stand up while the bus is in motion." "Don't put any part of your body out the window." "Don't fight." "Don't make messes."

These rules helped maintain order. But just because the rules were posted did not mean they were followed. When the rules were broken, there were consequences. The rules applied to everyone equally. I tried to be fair. Enforcing the rules was not the most enjoyable part of my job, but it was necessary. Having rules in place helped create an environment where everyone on the bus could experience a safe ride to school and a safe ride home. The rules made life more pleasant for everyone.

There is wisdom in observing rules. Rules such as those in the Ten Commandments give us boundaries, a common set of expectations, and limits on destructive behaviors, such as killing, adultery, stealing, lying, and coveting (desiring another person's possessions). Honoring our parents leads to life and is an act of thanksgiving toward those who brought us into the world. If everyone followed these rules, the world would look very different.

The commandments in today's Scripture instruct us about relationships. God is concerned with how we live together. But just because the rules are posted does not mean that they will be followed. When the rules are broken, we should name the wrongdoing and work for justice. God is concerned for our communities, and we should be, too.

Lord God, help me to see the Ten Commandments as a gift you have given to human beings, containing wisdom for how we are to live together. Help me to obey each of these commandments and extend the principles found here to the community of which I am a part. May I be a good neighbor and a messenger of your love. In Christ's name. Amen.

33. ANOTHER RIGHTEOUSNESS

In Christ I have a righteousness that is not my own and that
does not come from the Law but rather from the faithfulness
of Christ. It is the righteousness of God that is based on faith.
The righteousness that I have comes from knowing Christ, the
power of his resurrection, and the participation in his sufferings.
It includes being conformed to his death so that I may perhaps
reach the goal of the resurrection of the dead.
(Philippians 3:9b-11)

During my days as a college student, I remember being
approached by a group of teenagers. It was clear to me they were
on campus as part of a church group, and I guessed they were
given an assignment to engage someone in conversation. I was
right.

A young man asked, "Can you name the Ten Commandments?"
I was a religion major, and named them. He then said, "Do you
think it is always possible to keep them?" I said no. I know the Ten
Commandments are a powerful guide. However, in and of them-
selves, they cannot save me.

Though we should always strive to keep the "Ten Words," who
has not broken at least one? Have I always honored my parents?
Have I kept God first? Have I told the truth? Have I been content
with what I have?

The answer is no. But God in Christ has offered forgiveness when we fail and a form of righteousness that exceeds the Law. In Paul's words: "It is the righteousness of God that is based on faith." Our salvation is given in Jesus Christ, who has secured it through his life, death, and resurrection. By faith, Christ invites me to let him be my life, my righteousness, my everything. That invitation still stands.

Make the words of this great Irish hymn your own: "Be thou my vision, O Lord of my heart; / naught be all else to me, save that thou art. / Thou my best thought, by day or by night, / waking or sleeping, thy presence my light."[17] Place your faith in Jesus, and live by his love.

Lord Jesus, make me a new creature through faith in you. May I see that every good in me is your gift, a work of grace to be used for your service. Amen.

34. STAND IN AWE

Moses said to the people, "Don't be afraid, because God has come only to test you and to make sure you are always in awe of God so that you don't sin." The people stood at a distance while Moses approached the thick darkness in which God was present. (Exodus 20:20-21)

Have you ever wanted to quit sinning?

If you are a Christian, surely you must have this desire. But how to accomplish it? As Dallas Willard asked, "How can ordinary human beings such as you and I...follow and become like Jesus Christ?...How can we be like him not as a pose or by a constant and grinding effort, but with the ease and power he had—flowing from the inner depths, acting with quiet force from the innermost mind and soul of the Christ who has become a real part of us?"[18]

In today's Scripture, Moses offers us a clue: "God has come... to test you and to make sure you are always in awe of God so that you don't sin." The people, after an encounter with God, stand in awe. Awe of God is a sin-repellent.

Discovering the absolute, unparalleled goodness and beauty of God is an essential step if we don't want to sin. Compared with God, sin looks unattractive. So think about the character of God, the actions of God, and the stories of God that you have read or heard from the Bible.

With close friends or family, discuss what you know of God. In the margins of this book write a few words that come to mind: What is it about God that is worthy of our worship? When we say God is good, what do we mean and how do we know? What has God accomplished on our behalf that makes God worthy of our worship?

Making such a list will help you on your way to holiness. God will be the fuel that propels the engine of faithfulness, helping you keep God's commands. The Lord will embrace you, the Holy Spirit will guide you, and Jesus Christ will be your teacher. You're in good hands.

Stand in awe.

God Almighty, I have struggled with sin. I want to stop. Help! I trust you will. May I see you as you are—loving, faithful, and just—and serve you with all I am. Amen.

35. LIVING THE STORY

If you are reading these devotions as a family, use the ideas and activities in the Small Talk children's handout for this week. If you are reading the devotions alone, as a couple, or in a small group, you are invited to take up two practices: prayer and confession. These practices will challenge you and enable you to grow as a follower of Christ. They will create space where God can transform you, speak to you, guide you, and teach you, by the power of the Holy Spirit.

Prayer

Prayer is conversation with God. This week, tell God what is on your mind, and listen to what God has to say. Thinking carefully about the Ten Commandments may have led you to consider matters in your own life, such as your obedience to God. You may have discovered a deep desire to live more faithfully as Jesus' disciple.

For some, keeping a prayer journal may help. For others, you may wish to use written prayers or the words of the Bible, such as the Psalms. Both spontaneous prayers and written prayers can be used by God to move and reshape our hearts.

Confession

I have heard people say, "I am not perfect," but when asked where they are lacking, few of them are willing or able to respond. Identifying and sharing our failings is difficult. The regular practice of confession, however, is commanded in the Bible (for example, in 1 John 1:8-9) and helps us grow in holiness.

Tell God where you fall short. God already knows, and you are already forgiven! As you confess your sins, you are reassured of Christ's grace, and Christ is there to help you as you seek to grow beyond your present struggle.

If you wish to take confession a step further, sit down with a pastor or trusted friend and ask if that person will hear your confession. When you finish, the person can say, "Your sins are forgiven," because they are! Hearing someone else affirm this truth will reinforce it and remind you that confession binds the community together. When we as Christians know that others around us fail and have weaknesses, we become more generous and slower to judge.

Week Six
THE GREAT COMMANDMENT

Deuteronomy 6:1-9

36. REMEMBER THE STORY

Now these are the commandments, the regulations, and the case laws that the LORD your God commanded me to teach you to follow in the land you are entering to possess, so that you will fear the LORD your God by keeping all his regulations and his commandments that I am commanding you—both you and your sons and daughters—all the days of your life and so that you will lengthen your life. Listen to them, Israel! Follow them carefully so that things will go well for you and so that you will continue to multiply exactly as the LORD, your ancestors' God, promised you, in a land full of milk and honey. (Deuteronomy 6:1-3)

The Book of Deuteronomy reads like a farewell speech of Moses, who reminds the Israelites about all they have learned while wandering in the wilderness. Just over Moses' shoulder is the land of promise, where they will wage war, settle, grow crops, care for livestock, raise families, and, Moses hopes, live in faithfulness to God. In Deuteronomy 6, Moses urges his hearers to remain true to the Lord and the Lord's commandments.

The contents of the Bible, and the faith they are meant to inspire, are easy to forget. This is why the study of Scripture is so important. Scripture contains the commands, poems, history, and stories that assist us in living as faithful disciples of Jesus Christ. We draw on the contents of Scripture to reinforce our imaginations, so that when we are faced with daily challenges, we can respond in a manner that is aligned with God's story.

For example, if we encounter injustice we may recall Micah 6:8: "He has told you, human one, what is good and what the LORD requires from you: to do justice, embrace faithful love, and walk humbly with your God." When tempted to judge people on their looks, we can remember 1 Samuel 16:7: "God doesn't look at things like humans do. Humans see only what is visible to the eyes, but the LORD sees into the heart." If someone acts violently against us, either with words or fists, we might remember Jesus' words in Matthew 5:39: "If people slap you on your right cheek, you must turn the left cheek to them as well."

Spend time today reading your Bible, and dedicate yourself to making it a regular practice.

Lord, today I ask you to make me a student of the Bible, so that I might live faithfully according to the story found within it. Amen.

37. LISTEN!

Israel, listen! Our God is the LORD! Only the LORD! Love the LORD your God with all your heart, all your being, and all your strength. These words that I am commanding you today must always be on your minds. (Deuteronomy 6:4-6)

Every evening before dinner, my family joins hands and my three-year-old daughter leads us in prayer: "God is great, God is good, let us thank him for our food." This prayer reminds us that our food is a gift, from field to table. God is our provider; we owe thanks. Routine prayer establishes a rhythm and grounds us.

For the people of Israel, today's Scripture served a similar function. These words, known as the *Shema* ("Listen!" or "Hear!") are a declaration of faith in the One God, the God who rescued Israel from slavery. Still recited today, it is one of the most important prayers in the Jewish tradition.

Our passage today also includes these familiar words: "Love the LORD your God with all your heart, all your being, and all your strength." Jesus, when asked the greatest commandment, drew his response from these words, saying "You must love the Lord your God with all your heart, with all your being, and with all your mind." He added, "The second is like it: You must love your neighbor as you love yourself" (Matthew 22:37-39).

Loving God is a lifelong quest. The Book of Deuteronomy tells us to love God with heart, being, and strength. Jesus adds mind. True devotion requires everything. On our best days we give every effort over to God. But if we're honest, we can recall moments when we lost discipline, committed sin, and failed to live as God calls us. Life with God is always calling us onward, to be more than we are, until the day we are glorified and perfected and made new.

Have you given your entire life to God? Though we may fall short in some ways, the good news is this: we are called to begin living today the life God has prepared for us in eternity, and God has supplied us with the grace, in Jesus Christ, to do it.

Jesus, you are my Lord, the one who saves me. Help me to love you with all my heart, being, strength, and mind. Amen.

38. WHICH COMMANDMENT IS GREATEST?

Jesus replied, "The most important one is Israel, listen! Our God is the one Lord, and you must love the Lord your God with all your heart, with all your being, with all your mind, and with all your strength. *The second is this,* You will love your neighbor as yourself. *No other commandment is greater than these."*
(Mark 12:29-31)

The Bible is a tremendous book, filled with commandments that tell us what to do and what not to do. Which one is the most important?

Fortunately for us, an expert in the law chose to ask Jesus that very question. Jesus then provided us with an insightful answer. "Our God is the one Lord, and you must love the Lord your God with all your heart, with all your being, with all your mind, and with all your strength." He added a second, to "love your neighbor as yourself."

Love God. Love people. Simple words that are challenging to apply yet are nevertheless an excellent guide. New Testament scholar Scot McKnight has gone so far as to label this two-pronged commandment the "Jesus Creed," pointing out that Christians would benefit greatly by daily praying and reciting these words of Jesus.[19]

Jesus' commandments instruct us in another way. He took both from the words of the Old Testament. The first you will recognize from Deuteronomy 6:4-5. The second is borrowed from Leviticus 19:18.

The New Testament documents do not replace the words of the Old Testament. Christians have long believed that God was at work before the coming of Christ and that what has gone before is important for what has been revealed. We believe that Jesus is not only the Messiah of the world, but first the Messiah of Israel. That is a claim Christians should make with humility.

God's story of salvation is a big story, full of twists and turns, major players and minor characters. You are called to be a part of it, learning and applying the wisdom found in the Old and New Testaments, as well as understanding the grand themes of the Bible.

Have you dedicated yourself to searching the Scriptures? Are you seeking to apply the "Jesus Creed" in your life? Both are critical for disciples of Jesus.

God Almighty, you are my teacher. May I live according to the words of Jesus: to love God and love people. Amen.

39. Pass the Story On

Recite them to your children. Talk about them when you are sitting around your house and when you are out and about, when you are lying down and when you are getting up. Tie them on your hand as a sign. They should be on your forehead as a symbol. Write them on your house's doorframes and on your city's gates. (Deuteronomy 6:7-9)

My home is filled with reminders. I have a photo album that tells the story of my wedding. On my desk I have pictures of my daughter that make me smile. I have diplomas on the wall of my study and a certificate from my ordination to the ministry on top of a bookshelf. A Texas flag is pinned to the ceiling above my chair.

These items call to mind experiences, people, stories, and aspects of my identity that guide me in daily decisions and reinforce elements of my character.

Today's Scripture imparted a similar message to Israelites: the story of Israel needs to be passed on, not only on special occasions but also in the normal, everyday moments of life. Our text encouraged the people of Israel to have physical reminders—a cord held in the hand, a *phylactery* upon the forehead, a sign on the door or the city gates—but also to tell the stories.

For the people first hearing these words, the stories would have included the plagues in Egypt, the deliverance at the Red Sea, the wanderings in the wilderness with God's provision of manna and quail, and the giving of the law. For us, those stories are only a beginning. We are also called to tell our children and friends our stories of life with God, such as how we came to hear about Jesus and how our lives have changed.

Tonight, share a meal with people you love and tell stories of the faith. Ask the people if they have a favorite Bible story, and give them a chance to tell it in their own words. Then share personal stories of how God has been at work in your life and in the life of your family. You may wish to write some of the details in a journal.

You have been at work, O God. May I tell the stories of faith, from the Bible and from my life. In Christ's name. Amen.

40. No Hands But Yours

The person whose help is the God of Jacob—the person whose
hope rests on the LORD their God—is truly happy! God: the
maker of heaven and earth, the sea, and all that is in them,
God: who is faithful forever, who gives justice to people who
are oppressed, who gives bread to people who are starving! The
LORD: who frees prisoners. The LORD: who makes the blind see.
The LORD: who straightens up those who are bent low. The LORD:
who loves the righteous. The LORD: who protects immigrants,
who helps orphans and widows, but who makes the way of the
wicked twist and turn! (Psalm 146:5-9)

This passage from the Psalms captures many themes of the
Bible. God is named as the creator, the faithful one, the cham-
pion of the oppressed, and the one who feeds the starving. God
frees prisoners, gives sight to the blind, and protects foreigners,
orphans, and widows. But how does God do it?

There is a story about a statue of Jesus that had stood for many
years in a church. The hands of the statue had been destroyed, and
the people of the church discussed restoration. In the end, they
decided to leave the statue as it was, in order to communicate a
message. Borrowing a line from a poem attributed to St. Teresa of
Ávila, they fixed a sign below the statue: "Christ has no hands but
yours."

When our hope rests in the Lord, we can't help being involved in the things he does. Jesus understood this. Standing in a synagogue in Nazareth, Jesus read from the Isaiah scroll, "The Spirit of the Lord is upon me, because the Lord has anointed me. He has sent me to preach good news to the poor, to proclaim release to the prisoners and recovery of sight to the blind, to liberate the oppressed, and to proclaim the year of the Lord's favor" (Luke 4:18-19). As the Gospel of Luke unfolds and we see Jesus working in the world, we realize exactly what he meant.

Jesus taught his disciples to be about that same work. Indeed, Paul refers to Christians as "Christ's body." It seems we've been made part of God's work.

So, trust in God. Love God. And show it by dedicating your life to God's work in the world.

Lord God, may I be happy in you and take part in your work. Amen.

41. WHERE DO I BEGIN?

But Ruth replied, "Don't urge me to leave you or to turn back
from you. Where you go I will go, and where you stay I will stay.
Your people will be my people and your God my God. Where
you die I will die, and there I will be buried. May the LORD deal
with me, be it ever so severely, if even death separates you and
me." When Naomi realized that Ruth was determined to go with
her, she stopped urging her. (Ruth 1:16-18 NIV)

The commandment to love God with all we have and all we are
should bear real fruit in our lives. What do others see when they
behold your life and your character?

What did Ruth see in Naomi?

In today's Scripture, we read of Ruth's choice to cast her lot
with Naomi and Naomi's God. Maybe Ruth had heard Naomi pray
the *Shema* morning and evening or tell stories of Moses and the
people being delivered from slavery in Egypt. Maybe Ruth saw
Naomi following God's commandments to protect the foreigner,
the widow, and the orphan. Maybe Ruth witnessed Naomi's devotion to God in the face of hardship.

What would your life be like if you had heard the commandment to love God with all you have, and you had *lived* it?

The stories of Scripture teach us how to play our part in the
story of what God has done, and is doing, in our world. These truly

are stories you should know. More important than that, they are stories you should live.

You may say, "But I don't know all the stories yet!" Elton Trueblood responds, "We do not have to wait until we know the whole truth about anything to make our witness. If we were to wait for this, we should wait forever."[20] The better question, then, is "Where do I begin?"

Begin with love of God. Show that love through love of your neighbor. Extend a kind word. Find a place that serves the needy, then give time and presence. Forgive someone you have held a grudge against. Make a commitment to pray as you begin each day. Start where you are. And keep going.

Lord, may I love you, as your grace allows. May I show this every day through my actions, and may you keep me on my journey as a disciple of Christ. In his name. Amen.

42. Living the Story

If you are reading these devotions as a family, use the ideas and activities in the Small Talk children's handout for this week. If you are reading the devotions alone, as a couple, or in a small group, you are invited to take up two practices: margin and slowness. These practices will challenge you and enable you to grow as a follower of Christ. They will create space where God can transform you, speak to you, guide you, and teach you, by the power of the Holy Spirit.

Margin

Look at this page. Surrounding the text, you find open space called "margin." The margin helps you focus on what is important—the text itself—and devote your full energy to the message.

Now, think of your life. Do you have margin? Is there space between and around your activities? Or are you constantly busy, hurrying from place to place?

Busyness and hurry are two of the biggest obstacles to our growth and development as Christians. We take pride in saying we are busy, but a better approach is to maintain a consistent, healthy pace.

Take a look at your calendar and see what you can eliminate in order to add margin. Do not schedule appointments back to back, but instead allow for a natural break. In that space, listen for God, and ask how you might better observe the "Greatest Commandment" during your next commitment.

Slowness

Learning the stories of the Bible and growing in the Christian life take time! Yet often we expect these things to happen over-night, as though by the next morning we can exist as sinless human beings. You'll find that embracing the fact that growth is slow and often imperceptible will allow you to release a great deal of guilt and restlessness.

This week, as a reminder that growth in holiness takes time, slow down. Look for God in spare moments. Pick the longest line at the store. Stay in the slow lane on the highway. Chew your food more slowly. Enjoy things you would have missed otherwise.

God is calling you onward. Keep going! But go slowly.

NOTES

1. Howard G. Hendricks and William D. Hendricks, *Living by the Book: The Art and Science of Reading the Bible* (Chicago: Moody, 1991), 27.

2. From Frost's letter to Louis Untermeyer, dated August 21, 1935. Quoted in *Living by the Book*, 216.

3. Dan B. Allender, *Sabbath* (Nashville: Thomas Nelson, 2009), 5.

4. Joshua Choonmin Kang, *Scripture by Heart: Devotional Practices for Memorizing God's Word* (Downers Grove, IL: InterVarsity, 2010. Kindle Edition.), location 133 of 1319.

5. Jonathan Lemire, "Victoria Ruvolo, who was hit by turkey nearly 6 years ago, forgives teens for terrible prank," *New York Daily News Online*, http://articles.nydailynews.com /2010-11-07/local/27080547_1_victoria-ruvolo-ryan-cushing-forgives.

6. In mathematical contexts, the ">" symbol indicates that the value on the left side of an equation *is greater than* the value on the right side, for example, $10 > 5$.

7. George Herbert, "Gratefulness," in *The Complete English Poems* (New York: Penguin Books, 2004. Kindle Edition.), location 4114 of 12107.

8. Kelso Carter, "Standing on the Promises," *The United Methodist Hymnal* (Nashville: The United Methodist Publishing House, 1989), 374.

9. Dietrich Bonhoeffer, *The Cost of Discipleship* (New York: Macmillan, 1963), 99.

10. W. Reginald Ward and Richard P. Heitzenrater, eds., *The Works of John Wesley, Volume 18: Journals and Diaries I (1735-1738)* (Nashville: Abingdon, 1988), 242.

11. Ambrosiaster, from his *Commentary on Paul's Epistles,* as quoted in *Ancient Christian Commentary on Scripture, New Testament VI: Romans* (Downers Grove, IL: InterVarsity, 1998), 121.

12. Søren Kierkegaard, *Fear and Trembling / Repetition,* edited and translated by Howard V. Hong and Edna H. Hong (Princeton, NJ: Princeton University Press, 1983).

13. Louis Albert Banks, ed., *Spurgeon's Illustrative Anecdotes* (New York: Funk & Wagnalls, 1906), 121-22.
14. Dallas Willard, *The Divine Conspiracy: Rediscovering Our Hidden Life in God* (San Francisco: HarperSanFrancisco, 1998), 56–57.
15. Timothy Keller, *Counterfeit Gods: The Empty Promises of Money, Sex, and Power, and the Only Hope That Matters* (New York: Dutton, 2009), xviii.
16. C. S. Lewis, *Mere Christianity* (San Francisco: HarperSanFrancisco, 2001), 189.
17. Eleanor H. Hull, "Be Thou My Vision," in *The United Methodist Hymnal* (Nashville: The United Methodist Publishing House, 1989), 451.
18. Dallas Willard, *The Spirit of the Disciplines: Understanding How God Changes Lives* (San Francisco: HarperSanFrancisco, 1988), 14.
19. Scot McKnight, *The Jesus Creed: Loving God, Loving Others* (Brewster, MA: Paraclete Press, 2004).
20. David Elton Trueblood, *The Company of the Committed* (New York: Harper & Brothers, 1961), 66.